CFA Institute

Your Complete Guide—2017

CFA® PROGRAM CHANGES

How the Curriculum Advances Industry Practice

ISBN 978-1-944250-36-2

10 9 8 7 6 5 4 3 2 1

ABOUT THE AUTHOR

Stephanie Williams, MBA, is a Strategic Business Consultant, author, and powerhouse behind Booked and Branded Publishing. With over a decade of experience spanning corporate sales, real estate investment, and entrepreneurship, she brings unmatched clarity and confidence to every project.

Her expertise lies in transforming ideas into income — whether through premium ghostwriting, powerful branding, or step-by-step business building systems. Stephanie holds an MBA with a concentration in entrepreneurship from the Jack Welch Management Institute and has helped hundreds of professionals glow up their brands from the inside out.

Through her signature publishing and consulting firm, Stephanie empowers aspiring CEOs to turn their hustle into legacy — with strategy, speed, and style.

Made in the USA
Las Vegas, NV
03 November 2026

57420360R00024

CONTENTS

CE Qualified Activity CFA Institute 1 CE credit, inclusive of 0.5 SER credit

Foreword: CFA Program Curriculum Reflects Modern Industry Practice

Congratulations on your interest in the 2017 curriculum updates to the CFA Program. Your interest demonstrates your curiosity, determination, and commitment to continuous learning regarding investment industry advances and modern investment strategies. Your dedication to upgrading your skills is exactly aligned with what Benjamin Graham succinctly referred to as "advancing the standards of the profession."

The CFA Program curriculum is constantly evolving. We update hundreds of pages each year to ensure our candidates are assessed against the most current core competencies expected of professionals. Sometimes the updates represent minor revisions; other times, they represent wholesale changes.

I have the privilege of speaking with our members frequently, and these conversations are enormously valuable. Many of you implore us to include recent industry developments that you are seeing and experiencing firsthand. I can assure you that these member insights positively influence the curriculum improvements. They also provide assurance that the curriculum already contains much of what you want and need.

Although informal conversations with members about curriculum are valuable, a defensible process demands a more systematic and holistic approach, which we call practice analysis. We ask practicing investment management professionals, university faculty, and regulators through panels, focus groups, online platforms, and surveys what critical competencies they believe are needed in an investment role today and how those should be translated into exam weights. I encourage you to volunteer to contribute to this process. Annual CFA Program curriculum updates are one way of assuring that the CFA charter—the credential you worked so hard to proudly earn—remains the gold standard. We want you, our members, to have ready and convenient access to the curriculum changes we make. In this way, you can easily maintain your professional competencies and step up your knowledge of the changing world around you.

Annual CFA Program curriculum updates are one way of assuring that the CFA charter—the credential you worked so hard to proudly earn—remains the gold standard.

We have identified 11 new areas for knowledge enhancement for 2017. All of the new readings in the CFA Program curriculum are being made available to you as part of your membership (that is, you don't have to pay for these!).

This represents the first in a series of annual updates we intend to provide to help members stay up-to-date with year-over-year changes in the CFA Program curriculum. You can also read how the curriculum has evolved over a longer time period. We are pleased you are endeavoring to upgrade your current knowledge base.

Thank you, and study on!

Stephen Horan, CFA, CIPM
Managing Director, Credentialing

How Has the CFA Program Curriculum Changed?

When did you obtain your CFA charter? Prior to the global financial crisis, whose lessons reinforced the importance of identifying and managing risk? Before the advent of traders using advanced computer networks to buy or sell stocks in fractions of a second? These are just two examples of how the investment management industry has changed dramatically in the past decade.

In an ever-evolving profession, it's more important than ever for investment managers to keep their finger on the pulse of not only industry trends but also the way that the CFA Program curriculum is constantly updated to meet the changing demands of the investment management business. Curriculum updates are not only for candidates; CFA Institute members can use these resources to expand their technical knowledge and reinforce their commitment to high ethical standards.

CFA Program curriculum changes/updates for 2017 reflect advances in skills that are necessary to meet the needs of clients. As part of the global practice analysis process, investment management professionals noted the importance of three primary areas: ethics, risk management, and expansion of the investment decision-making process to incorporate ESG (environmental, social, and governance) factors. Several curriculum readings update the current state of the industry with respect to these areas and discuss the associated competencies required to successfully practice.

Ethics remains the unifying theme that links investment professionals throughout the world. Closing the apparent "trust gap" requires not only knowledge of an ethical standard but also a devotion to incorporating ethical principles into everyday practice. The new ethics readings reinforce these challenges through the use of practical, client-based cases.

The continued globalization of capital markets has led to increased investor uncertainty and, in turn, a demand for more sophisticated risk measurement models.

The continued globalization of capital markets has led to increased investor uncertainty and, in turn, a demand for more sophisticated risk measurement models. Advances in measuring and managing market risk are explored in several 2017 curriculum readings.

Corporate governance continues to be a fundamental driver of portfolio performance. Over the last few years, risk factors related to a firm's social and environmental profile—the Volkswagen emissions scandal serves as a prime example—have become economically material. As a result, a core skill required of investment advisers is the ability to integrate ESG factors into the portfolio construction process. The new Level I reading represents a significant advance in the coverage of ESG factors in the CFA Program.

2017 CFA PROGRAM REFRESHER READING, LEVEL I

Standards, Ethics, and Regulations

Revisiting the Importance of Ethical Behavior

CFA Institute members are both expected and required to meet high ethical standards at all times as they work within their chosen profession. This material reintroduces ideas and concepts that will help you fully understand ethics (behavior using a guiding set of moral principles and rules of conduct) and the importance of ethical behavior within the investment industry. This reading presents various types of ethical issues commonly encountered within the investment profession, as well as be reintroduced to the CFA Institute Code of Ethics. Subsequently, you will be reminded of how to identify challenges to ethical behavior, distinguish between rules-based legal and ethical standards, and apply the ethics framework to your decision-making process.

Applicable Reading:

"Ethics and Trust in the Investment Profession"

By Bidhan L. Parmar, PhD (USA), Dorothy C. Kelly, CFA, at McIntire School of Commerce, and David B. Stevens, CFA (USA)

Economics

A Deeper Understanding of Demand and Supply

Economics is the study of production, distribution, and consumption and is divided into two study areas: macroeconomics, which explores aggregate economic qualities on a national level, and microeconomics, which explains markets and decision making among consumers and businesses at the more individual level. The material will review the *theory of the consumer*, which delves into the demand for goods and services, and the *theory of the firm*, which looks at the supply of goods and services by firms. This material will examine such factors that affect economic concepts as price, income, and elements of demand; explain the product of labor; distinguish between normal goods and inferior goods; and describe how economies of scale affect costs.

Applicable Reading:

"Topics in Demand and Supply Analysis"

By Richard V. Eastin, PhD at the University of Southern California (USA), and Gary L. Arbogast, PhD, CFA (USA)

Corporate Finance

Understanding Corporate Governance and ESG Factors

This material will help you identify and analyze weak corporate governance, the problems it has caused (e.g., accounting scandals, bankruptcies), and how it significantly contributed to the 2008–09 global financial crisis. Regulations have since been introduced with the goal of promoting strong corporate governance practices among companies and protecting markets and investors. This material will reinforce the importance of good corporate principles and practices while explaining the basic needs, functions, and influence of different stakeholder groups. The reading will also explain the importance and mechanisms behind stakeholder management (e.g., boards of directors, the audit function, policies on remuneration) and the increasing integration of ESG factors as the basis for good corporate governance practices within companies.

Applicable Reading:

"Corporate Governance and ESG: An Introduction"

By Assem Safieddine, PhD, at Suliman S. Olayan Business School, American University of Beirut (Lebanon), Young Lee, CFA (USA), Donna F. Anderson, CFA (USA), and Deborah Kidd, CFA, at Boyd Watterson Asset Management, LLC (USA)

2017 CFA PROGRAM REFRESHER READING, LEVEL II

Financial Statement Analysis

The Basic Framework, Techniques, and Case Studies

Applicable Reading:

"Integration of Financial Statement Analysis Techniques"

By Jack T. Ciesielski, Jr., CPA, CFA, at R.G. Associates, Inc., publisher of the Analyst's Accounting Observer (USA)

The purpose of financial analysis is to assist with important economic and investment decision making. Such financial analysis increases the visibility and/or chance of a favorable investment outcome. This material, through the use of case studies, is designed to explore the effective use of financial analysis across different types of companies using a basic framework that describes the purpose of the analysis and how to collect data, process data into useful metrics, interpret data, develop and communicate conclusions/recommendations, and perform a follow-up reassessment. This reading will also address how changes in accounting standards/methods and balance sheet modifications affect a company's most current financial condition.

Derivatives I

The How-To of Pricing and Valuation of Forward Contracts

Applicable Reading:

"Pricing and Valuation of Forward Commitments"

By Robert E. Brooks, PhD, CFA, at the University of Alabama (USA), and Barbara Valbuzzi, CFA (Italy)

Derivatives of all types have become a valued and mainstream investment product. This material will introduce you to the method of pricing and valuing derivative instruments known as forward commitments—that is, contracts providing the ability to lock in a price/rate at which one can buy/sell the underlying instrument at a future date or exchange an agreed-upon amount of money at a future series of dates. This reading provides the foundation for understanding how forwards, futures, and swaps are priced and valued and for understanding and calculating the no-arbitrage value for equity, interest rate, fixed-income, and currency forward and futures contracts, as well as equity, interest rate, and currency swaps.

Derivatives II

A Better Understanding of Options Valuations

Applicable Reading:

"Valuation of Contingent Claims"

By Robert E. Brooks, PhD, CFA, at the University of Alabama (USA), and David Maurice Gentle, MEc, BSc, CFA, at Omega Risk Consulting (Australia)

Options, a type of contingent claim, are becoming more popular within the investment industry. In addition, many investments today contain embedded options. An option gives the owner the right, but not the obligation, to a payoff determined by an underlying asset, rate, or other derivative instrument. This reading will provide you with an understanding of how the values of options are determined using two different option valuation models: the continuous-time Black–Scholes–Merton (BSM) model and the discrete-time binomial model. This material includes an exploration of valuations for American-style options and European-style options and of how common Greek metrics (e.g., delta, gamma, rho, and vega) are used.

Derivatives III

Strategies for Using Derivatives to Modify Risk and/or Return

Derivatives have become very useful investment tools, and many practitioners can benefit from a better understanding of the strategies behind their use in connection with a well-defined investment objective. There are many ways in which investors and financial managers routinely use a spectrum of derivative instruments to implement market strategies, take speculative positions, provide protection against future adverse events, or modify risk. This reading will illustrate ways in which derivatives (including call options, forward contracts, futures, and varying swap contracts) may be used in investment cases, such as to benefit a corporate treasury or protect a portfolio. It will also explain how to use covered calls to generate income, create a synthetic long position, deploy a protective put, and structure a bull spread/bear spread and why collars, calendar spreads, and straddles are used.

Applicable Reading:

"Derivatives Strategies"

By Robert A. Strong, PhD, CFA, at the University of Maine (USA), and Russell A. Rhoads, CFA, at The Options Institute at CBOE (USA)

Alternative Investments

Commodities and Commodity Derivatives 101

Commodities—physical goods that are attributable to natural resources and that can be traded in physical (spot) and futures and forward markets—have become popular alternative investments over the past several years. They can include energy, grains, industrial and precious metals, livestock, and agricultural crops. Commodities offer the potential for portfolio diversification because of their historically low correlation with stocks and bonds and their inflation-hedging qualities. This reading provides you with explanation of the life cycles and characteristics of commodities as well as valuations for commodities and commodity-derived contracts. It also explores the operations of commodity exchanges, which allow for price discovery and risk transfer. You will learn about the commodity trading environment and its common trading participants, explore the three theories of futures returns, and understand the key differentiating characteristics among popular commodity indexes.

Applicable Reading:

"Commodities and Commodity Derivatives: An Introduction"

David Burkart, CFA, is at Coloma Capital Futures, LLC (USA). James Alan Finnegan, RMA, CFA (USA).

Risk Management

Understanding Value at Risk and Other Scenario Measures

Risk continues to be a four-letter word. Identifying, measuring, and managing market risk—the risk arising from changes in the markets because of movement in stock prices, interest rates, exchange rates, and commodity prices—is vitally important. Managing market risk relies heavily on the use of models that attempt to capture elements of prices as well as market sensitivities. But investment industry practitioners must also be savvy regarding deploying such models as value at risk (VaR)—understanding and appreciating their strengths and limitations and identifying when to supplement with another model/approach. This reading will explain and explore the various aspects and three methods of estimating VaR, the use of and reasons for stress tests, historical and hypothetical scenarios, and other risk tools. This material will also teach you about common industry risk constraints, such as risk budgets, position limits, scenario limits, stop-loss limits, and capital allocation.

Applicable Reading:

"Measuring and Managing Market Risk"

By Don M. Chance, PhD, CFA, at Louisiana State University (USA), and Michelle McCarthy at Nuveen (USA)

Portfolio Management
Understanding Value at Risk and Other Scenario Measures

Applicable Reading:

"Algorithmic Trading and High-Frequency Trading"

By John Bates, PhD, at Judge Business School, University of Cambridge (United Kingdom)

Technological advancements have allowed multi-asset-class execution algorithms and high-frequency trading algorithms to flourish as market transactions get faster and more competitive. But there are concerns among market participants and regulators that this new technology is or will be severely disruptive. With an estimated 75% of US stock trades now bypassing humans and being executed by computers, practitioners will need to better understand the new world order of market transactions. This reading will teach you about the two main types of algorithms and their purposes, the life cycle of an algorithm (e.g., alpha discovery, new pattern identification, implementation, backtesting, production, and tuning), and how surveillance algorithms can be used to identify potential market abuses and compliance breaches. You can also explore the positive and negative effects of using algorithms.

2017 CFA PROGRAM REFRESHER READING, LEVEL III

Private Wealth Management
Understanding and Preparing for Life-Cycle Finance for Individuals

Applicable Reading:

"Risk Management for Individuals"

By David M. Blanchett, CFP, CFA, at Morningstar Investment Management (USA), David M. Cordell, PhD, CFP, CFA, at the University of Texas at Dallas (USA), Michael S. Finke, PhD, at Texas Tech University (USA), and Thomas M. Idzorek, CFA, at Morningstar (USA)

Risk management for individuals is a key element of life-cycle finance—the concept of helping investors achieve their goals over various stages of their life cycle, including meeting retirement income goals. It recognizes that as investors age and move out of one phase and into the next, the fundamental nature of their total wealth evolves, as do the risks that they face. It logically takes a holistic view of the individual's financial situation as he or she moves through life. Individuals are exposed to a range of risks over their full life cycle. A sound and well-constructed plan for risk management will include the selection of investment products and strategies that can mitigate the risk of future shortfalls and will mesh with an individual's financial goals. This reading will explore the two primary asset types, the seven financial stages of life, the four key steps in the risk management process, the various forms of risk individuals potentially face, the considerations for selecting between fixed and variable annuities, and the impact of determining risk tolerance levels.

What Happens behind the Scenes at CFA Institute?

We continuously update the CFA Program curriculum by connecting directly with practicing investment management professionals, university faculty, and regulators to ask them what critical knowledge, skills, and abilities they believe are needed in an investment role today. This process, called practice analysis, is a dynamic assessment method that informs updates to the CFA Program curriculum.

CONTINUOUS PRACTITIONER INPUT

Potential changes come from a wide variety of sources: CFA Program candidates, university professors, prep providers, and others. These typically minor changes reflect areas for potential improvement or enhanced clarity. Additionally, CFA Institute curriculum staff monitor for environmental changes that affect the industry and practices. For example, if accounting standards change, the curriculum is revised to reflect the new standards and their potential effects on companies' financial statements. The curriculum also often includes examples based on real information and economic history and references companies, regulators, regulations, and more to demonstrate concepts. The CFA Program curriculum is gradually updated as companies merge, regulatory bodies and regulations change, and economic history unfolds. Curriculum staff works with external parties to implement these changes.

MAJOR AND MINOR REVISIONS ENSURE RELEVANCY

Major revisions—such as a change of coverage across a topic area, major rewrites/replacements of entire readings, or the addition of new readings—are intended to ensure that the CFA Program curriculum maintains its relevance and stays up-to-date with current investment industry practice. Major revisions result primarily from two sources: practice analysis and general recognition that coverage of some topic in the curriculum is outdated or needs improvement.

Practice analysis identifies emerging or new trends in the investment industry, updates the Candidate Body of Knowledge (CBOK), and points to gaps in the current curriculum. Practice analysis may identify the need for minor revisions, but it is oriented toward macro changes in the industry and its environment.

PRIORITIZING REVISIONS AND TAKING NEXT STEPS

When a need for a major revision has been identified, the CFA Institute curriculum staff work with a variety of external parties to prioritize and plan revisions. These external parties include industry practitioners who work with curriculum staff on an

ongoing basis (curriculum level advisers, or CLAs), subject matter experts (SMEs), and a working body of industry practitioners and academics (working body). Initially, major revisions are prioritized, and an overall revision plan is scheduled.

Next, curriculum staff and CLAs meet with SMEs globally for "practice intensives"—that is, working meetings designed to develop learning outcome statements (LOS) that are well aligned with how concepts are thought about and used in practice. Practice intensives are intended to make the identified needs for major revisions actionable. In consultation with the CLAs, curriculum staff take the information from the practice intensives and develop reading planning documents that are designed to guide the external individuals authoring new readings. Members of the working body may be surveyed to confirm that the LOS and reading planning documents reflect current acceptable practices. Numerous consultants—industry practitioners and academics—review each reading to ensure that it satisfies the desired learning outcomes, reflects current global industry practice, and applies sound teaching practices before it is considered complete and ready for the curriculum.

Through this multistep system, CFA Institute maintains a systematic, practitioner-based process for keeping the program relevant.

EARN CE CREDITS

Remaining up-to-date with changes made to the CFA Program curriculum is an important component of keeping current with the knowledge and skills needed in an investment role today. Because we believe in a commitment to lifelong learning, we see these updates as valuable for CFA Institute members who wish to keep current or those who need a "refresher" on certain topics or methods.

CFA Institute members who read the curriculum update information included here may claim 1 CE credit, including 0.5 SER credits, using their online CE tracking tool. Claim this credit via your online tracker at https://www.cfainstitute.org/learning/continuinged/ce/members/pages/index.aspx.

Individual readings—available as an exclusive member benefit via the CFA Program Curriculum Updates: Refresher Readings collection—qualify for the following CE credits, which also may be claimed using the online CE tracking tool:

- Ethics and Trust in the Investment Profession (1 CE/1 SER) https://www.cfainstitute.org/learning/products/publications/readings/Pages/ethics_and_trust_in_the_investment_profession__2017_.aspx
- Topics in Demand and Supply Analysis (1 CE) https://www.cfainstitute.org/learning/products/publications/readings/Pages/topics_in_demand_and_supply_analysis__2017_.aspx
- Corporate Governance and ESG: An Introduction (1 CE/1 SER) https://www.cfainstitute.org/learning/products/publications/readings/Pages/corporate_governance_and_esg__an_introduction__2017_.aspx
- Integration of Financial Statement Analysis Techniques (1.5 CE) https://www.cfainstitute.org/learning/products/publications/readings/Pages/integration_of_financial_statement_analysis_techniques__2017_.aspx
- Pricing and Valuation of Forward Commitments (2 CE) https://www.cfainstitute.org/learning/products/publications/readings/Pages/pricing_and_valuation_of_forward_commitments__2017_.aspx
- Valuation of Contingent Claims (2 CE) https://www.cfainstitute.org/learning/products/publications/readings/Pages/valuation_of_contingent_claims__2017_.aspx
- Derivatives Strategies (1.5 CE) https://www.cfainstitute.org/learning/products/publications/readings/Pages/derivatives_strategies__2017_.aspx
- Commodities and Commodity Derivatives: An Introduction (1.5 CE) https://www.cfainstitute.org/learning/products/publications/readings/Pages/commodities_and_commodity_derivatives__an_introduction__2017_.aspx
- Measuring and Managing Market Risk (1.5 CE) https://www.cfainstitute.org/learning/products/publications/readings/Pages/measuring_and_managing_market_risk__2017_.aspx
- Algorithmic Trading and High-Frequency Trading (0.5 CE) https://www.cfainstitute.org/learning/products/publications/readings/Pages/algorithmic_trading_and_high-frequency_trading__2017_.aspx
- Risk Management for Individuals (2.5 CE) https://www.cfainstitute.org/learning/products/publications/readings/Pages/risk_management_for_individuals__2017_.aspx

Standards, Ethics, and Regulations

Ethics and Trust in the Investment Profession

by Bidhan L. Parmar, PhD, Dorothy C. Kelly, CFA, and David B. Stevens, CFA

Bidhan L. Parmar, PhD (USA). Dorothy C. Kelly, CFA, is at McIntire School of Commerce, University of Virginia (USA). David B. Stevens, CFA (USA).

LEARNING OUTCOMES

Mastery	*The candidate should be able to:*
☐	**a.** explain ethics;
☐	**b.** describe the role of a code of ethics in defining a profession;
☐	**c.** identify challenges to ethical behavior;
☐	**d.** describe the need for high ethical standards in the investment industry;
☐	**e.** distinguish between ethical and legal standards;
☐	**f.** describe and apply a framework for ethical decision making.

INTRODUCTION

As a candidate in the CFA Program, you are both expected and required to meet high ethical standards. This reading introduces ideas and concepts that will help you understand the importance of ethical behavior in the investment industry. You will be introduced to various types of ethical issues within the investment profession and learn about the CFA Institute Code of Ethics. Subsequently, you will be introduced to a framework as a way to approach ethical decision making.

Imagine that you are employed in the research department of a large financial services firm. You and your colleagues spend your days researching, analyzing, and valuing the shares of publicly traded companies and sharing your investment recommendations with clients. You love your work and take great satisfaction in knowing that your recommendations can help the firm's investing clients make informed investment decisions that will help them meet their financial goals and improve their lives.

Several months after starting at the firm, you learn that an analyst at the firm has been terminated for writing and publishing research reports that misrepresented the fundamental risks of some companies to investors. You learn that the analyst wrote the reports with the goal of pleasing the management of the companies that were the subjects of the research reports. He hoped that these companies would hire your firm's investment banking division for its services and he would be rewarded with large bonuses for helping the firm increase its investment banking fees. Some clients bought shares based on the analyst's reports and suffered losses. They posted stories on the internet about their losses and the misleading nature of the reports. When the media investigated and published the story, the firm's reputation for investment research suffered. Investors began to question the firm's motives and the objectivity of its research recommendations. The firm's investment clients started to look elsewhere for investment advice, and company clients begin to transfer their business to firms with untarnished reputations. With business declining, management is forced to trim staff. Along with many other hard-working colleagues, you lose your job—through no fault of your own.

Imagine how you would feel in this situation. Most people would feel upset and resentful that their hard and honest work was derailed by someone else's unethical behavior. Yet, this type of scenario is not uncommon. Around the world, unsuspecting employees at such companies as SAC Capital, Stanford Financial Group, Everbright Securities, Enron, Satyam Computer Services, Arthur Andersen, and other large companies have experienced such career setbacks when someone else's actions destroyed trust in their companies and industries.

Businesses and financial markets thrive on trust—defined as a strong belief in the reliability of a person or institution. In a 2013 study on trust, investors indicated that to earn their trust, the top three attributes of an investment manager should be that it (1) has transparent and open business practices, (2) takes responsible actions to address an issue or crisis, and (3) has ethical business practices.[1] Although these attributes are valued by customers and clients in any industry, this reading will explore why they are of particular importance to the investment industry.

People may think that ethical behavior is simply about following laws, regulations, and other rules, but throughout our lives and careers we will encounter situations in which there is no definitive rule that specifies how to act, or the rules that exist may be unclear or even in conflict with each other. Responsible people, including investment professionals, must be willing and able to identify potential ethical issues and create solutions to them even in the absence of clearly stated rules.

SUMMARY

- Ethics refers to the study of making good choices. Ethics encompasses a set of moral principles and rules of conduct that provide guidance for our behavior.
- Situational influences are external factors that may shape our behavior.
- Challenges to ethical behavior include being overconfident in our own morality, underestimating the effect of situational influences, and focusing on the immediate rather than long-term outcomes or consequences of a decision.

1 CFA Institute and Edelman, "Investor Trust Study" (2013): http://www.cfapubs.org/doi/pdf/10.2469/ccb.v2013.n14.1.

- In any given profession, the code of ethics publicly communicates the established principles and expected behavior of its members.
- Members of a profession use specialized knowledge and skills to serve others; they share and agree to adhere to a common code of ethics to serve others and advance the profession.
- A code of ethics helps foster public confidence that members of the profession will use their specialized skills and knowledge to serve their clients and others.
- High ethical standards always matter and are of particular importance in the investment industry, which is based almost entirely on trust. Clients trust investment professionals to use their specialized skills and knowledge to serve clients and protect client assets. All stakeholders gain long-term benefits when investment professionals adhere to high ethical standards.
- Rules and laws often codify ethical actions that lead to better outcomes for society or specific groups of stakeholders.
- Organizations and individuals generally adhere to legal standards, but legal standards are often created to address past ethical failings and do not provide guidance for an evolving and increasingly complex world.
- Legal standards are often rule based. Ethical conduct goes beyond legal standards, balancing self-interest with the direct and indirect consequences of behavior on others.
- A framework for ethical decision making can help people look at and evaluate a decision from different perspectives, enabling them to identify important issues, make wise decisions, and limit unintended consequences.

Economics

Topics in Demand and Supply Analysis

by Richard V. Eastin, PhD, and Gary L. Arbogast, CFA

Richard V. Eastin, PhD, is at the University of Southern California (USA). Gary L. Arbogast, PhD, CFA (USA).

LEARNING OUTCOMES	
Mastery	*The candidate should be able to*
☐	**a.** calculate and interpret price, income, and cross-price elasticities of demand and describe factors that affect each measure;
☐	**b.** compare substitution and income effects;
☐	**c.** distinguish between normal goods and inferior goods;
☐	**d.** describe the phenomenon of diminishing marginal returns;
☐	**e.** determine and describe breakeven and shutdown points of production;
☐	**f.** describe how economies of scale and diseconomies of scale affect costs.

INTRODUCTION

In a general sense, *economics* is the study of production, distribution, and consumption and can be divided into two broad areas of study: macroeconomics and microeconomics. **Macroeconomics** deals with aggregate economic quantities, such as national output and national income, and is rooted in **microeconomics**, which deals with markets and decision making of individual economic units, including consumers and businesses. Microeconomics is a logical starting point for the study of economics.

Microeconomics classifies private economic units into two groups: consumers (or households) and firms. These two groups give rise, respectively, to the theory of the consumer and the theory of the firm as two branches of study. The *theory of the consumer* deals with consumption (the demand for goods and services) by utility-maximizing individuals (i.e., individuals who make decisions that maximize the satisfaction received from present and future consumption). The *theory of the firm* deals with the supply of goods and services by profit-maximizing firms.

It is expected that candidates will be familiar with the basic concepts of demand and supply. This material is covered in detail in the recommended prerequisite readings. In this reading, we will explore how buyers and sellers interact to determine transaction prices and quantities.

SUMMARY

This reading addressed several important concepts that extend the basic market model of demand and supply to assist the analyst in assessing a firm's breakeven and shutdown points of production. Demand concepts covered include own-price elasticity of demand, cross-price elasticity of demand, and income elasticity of demand. Supply concepts covered include total, average, and marginal product of labor; total, variable, and marginal cost of labor; and total and marginal revenue. These concepts are used to calculate the breakeven and shutdown points of production.

- Elasticity of demand is a measure of how sensitive quantity demanded is to changes in various variables.
- Own-price elasticity of demand is the ratio of percentage change in quantity demanded to percentage change in a good or service's own price.
- If own-price elasticity of demand is greater than one in absolute terms, demand is elastic and a decline in price will result in higher total expenditure on that good.
- If own-price elasticity of demand is less than one in absolute terms, demand is inelastic and a decline in price will result in a lower total expenditure on that good.
- If own-price elasticity of demand is equal to negative one, demand is unit, or unitary, elastic and total expenditure on that good is independent of price.
- Own-price elasticity of demand will almost always be negative.
- Income elasticity of demand is the ratio of the percentage change in quantity demanded to the percentage change in consumer income.
- Demand is negatively sloped because of either the substitution effect or the income effect.
- The substitution effect is the phenomenon in which, as a good's price falls, more of this good is substituted for other, more expensive goods.
- The income effect is the phenomenon in which, as a good's price falls, real income rises and, if this good is normal, more of it will be purchased.
- If the good is inferior, the income effect will partially or fully offset the substitution effect.
- There are two exceptions to the law of demand: Giffen goods and Veblen goods.
- Giffen goods are highly inferior and make up a large portion of the consumer budget. As price falls, the substitution effect tends to cause more of the good to be consumed, but the highly negative income effect overwhelms the substitution effect. Demand curves for Giffen goods are positively sloped.
- Veblen goods are highly valued high-priced "status" goods; consumers may tend to buy more of a good if its price rises.
- If income elasticity of demand is positive, the good is a normal good. If income elasticity of demand is negative, the good is an inferior good.
- Cross-price elasticity of demand is the ratio of the percentage change in quantity demanded of one good to the percentage change in the price of a related good.

- If cross-price elasticity between two goods is positive, they are substitutes, and if cross-price elasticity between two goods is negative, they are complements.
- The law of demand states that a decrease in price will cause an increase in quantity demanded.
- Total product of labor is a short-run concept that is the total quantity that is able to be produced for each level of labor input, holding all other inputs constant.
- Average product of labor (APL) is the total product of labor divided by number of labor hours.
- Marginal product of labor (MP_L) is the change in total product divided by the change in labor hours. MP_L might rise as more labor is added to a fixed amount of capital.
- The law of diminishing returns dictates that additional output must fall as more and more labor is added to a fixed amount of capital.
- Production costs increase as input prices rise and fall as inputs become more productive.
- Short-run total cost (STC) is the total expenditure on fixed capital plus the total expenditure on labor.
- Short-run marginal cost (SMC) equals the ratio of wage to marginal product of labor (MP_L).
- Average variable cost (AVC) is the ratio of wage to average product of labor (APL).
- Average total cost (ATC) is total cost (TC) divided by the number of units produced.
- Revenue is price times quantity sold.
- Marginal revenue (MR) is the ratio of change in revenue to change in output.
- Firms under conditions of perfect competition have no pricing power and, therefore, face a perfectly horizontal demand curve at the market price. For firms under conditions of perfect competition, price is identical to marginal revenue (MR).
- Firms under conditions of imperfect competition face a negatively sloped demand curve and have pricing power. For firms under conditions of imperfect competition, marginal revenue (MR) is less than price.
- Economic profit equals total revenue (TR) minus total economic cost, whereas accounting profit equals TR minus total accounting cost.
- Economic cost takes into account the total opportunity cost of all factors of production.
- Opportunity cost is the next best alternative forgone in making a decision.
- Maximum economic profit requires that (1) marginal revenue (MR) equals marginal cost (MC) and (2) MC not be falling with output.
- The breakeven point occurs when total revenue (TR) equals total cost (TC), otherwise stated as the output quantity at which average total cost (ATC) equals price.
- The shutdown point occurs when a firm is better off not operating than continuing to operate.
- If all fixed costs are sunk costs, then the shutdown point is when the market price falls below minimum average variable cost. At this price, the firm incurs only fixed cost and loses less money than when operating at a price that does not cover variable cost.

- In the short run, it may be rational for a firm to continue to operate while earning negative economic profit if operating losses would be greater than incurring only fixed costs.
- Economies of scale is defined as decreasing long-run cost per unit as output increases. Diseconomies of scale is defined as increasing long-run cost per unit as output increases.
- Long-run average total cost is the cost of production per unit of output under conditions in which all inputs are variable.
- Specialization efficiencies and bargaining power in input price can lead to economies of scale.
- Bureaucratic and communication breakdowns and bottlenecks that raise input prices can lead to diseconomies of scale.
- The minimum point on the long-run average total cost curve defines the minimum efficient scale for the firm.

Corporate Finance

Corporate Governance and ESG: An Introduction

by Assem Safieddine, PhD, Young Lee, CFA, Donna F. Anderson, CFA, and Deborah Kidd, CFA

Assem Safieddine, PhD, is at Suliman Olayan Business School, American University of Beirut (Lebanon). Young Lee, CFA (USA). Donna F. Anderson, CFA (USA). Deborah Kidd, CFA, is at Boyd Watterson Asset Management, LLC (USA).

LEARNING OUTCOMES

Mastery	*The candidate should be able to:*
☐	**a.** describe corporate governance;
☐	**b.** describe a company's stakeholder groups and compare interests of stakeholder groups;
☐	**c.** describe principal–agent and other relationships in corporate governance and the conflicts that may arise in these relationships;
☐	**d.** describe stakeholder management;
☐	**e.** describe mechanisms to manage stakeholder relationships and mitigate associated risks;
☐	**f.** describe functions and responsibilities of a company's board of directors and its committees;
☐	**g.** describe market and non-market factors that can affect stakeholder relationships and corporate governance;
☐	**h.** identify potential risks of poor corporate governance and stakeholder management and identify benefits from effective corporate governance and stakeholder management;
☐	**i.** describe factors relevant to the analysis of corporate governance and stakeholder management;
☐	**j.** describe environmental and social considerations in investment analysis;
☐	**k.** describe how environmental, social, and governance factors may be used in investment analysis.

INTRODUCTION

Weak corporate governance is a common thread found in many company failures. A lack of proper oversight by the board of directors, inadequate protection for minority shareholders, and incentives at companies that promote excessive risk taking are just a few of the examples that can be problematic for a company. Poor corporate governance practices resulted in several high-profile accounting scandals and corporate bankruptcies over the past several decades and have been cited as significantly contributing to the 2008–2009 global financial crisis.

In response to these company failures, regulations have been introduced to promote stronger governance practices and protect financial markets and investors. Academics, policy makers, and other groups have published numerous works discussing the benefits of good corporate governance and identifying core corporate governance principles believed to be essential to ensuring sound capital markets and the stability of the financial system.

The investment community has also demonstrated a greater appreciation for the importance of good corporate governance. The assessment of a company's corporate governance system, including consideration of conflicts of interest and transparency of operations, has increasingly become an essential factor in the investment decision-making process. Additionally, investors have become more attentive to environment and social issues related to a company's operations. Collectively, these areas often are referred to as environmental, social, and governance (**ESG**).

SUMMARY

The investment community has increasingly recognized the importance of corporate governance, as well as environmental and social considerations. Although practices concerning corporate governance (and ESG overall) will undoubtedly continue to evolve, investment analysts who have a good understanding of these concepts can better appreciate the implications of ESG in investment decision making. The core concepts covered in this reading are as follows:

- Corporate governance can be defined as a system of controls and procedures by which individual companies are managed.
- There are many systems of corporate governance, most reflecting the influences of either shareholder theory or stakeholder theory, or both. Current trends, however, point to increasing convergence.
- A corporation's governance system is influenced by several stakeholder groups, and the interests of the groups often diverge or conflict.
- The primary stakeholder groups of a corporation consist of shareholders, creditors, managers and employees, the board of directors, customers, suppliers, and government/regulators.
- A principal–agent relationship (or agency relationship) entails a principal hiring an agent to perform a particular task or service. In a corporate structure, such relationships often lead to conflicts among various stakeholders.

- Stakeholder management involves identifying, prioritizing, and understanding the interests of stakeholder groups and on that basis managing the company's relationships with stakeholders. The framework of corporate governance and stakeholder management reflects a legal, contractual, organizational, and governmental infrastructure.
- Mechanisms of stakeholder management may include general meetings, a board of directors, the audit function, company reporting and transparency, related-party transactions, remuneration policies (including say on pay), and other mechanisms to manage the company's relationship with its creditors, employees, customers, suppliers, and regulators.
- A board of directors is the central pillar of the governance structure, serves as the link between shareholders and managers, and acts as the shareholders' internal monitoring tool within the company.
- The structure and composition of a board of directors vary across countries and companies. The number of directors may vary, and the board typically includes a mix of expertise levels, backgrounds, and competencies.
- Executive (internal) directors are employed by the company and are typically members of senior management. Non-executive (external) directors have limited involvement in daily operations but serve an important oversight role.
- Two primary duties of a board of directors are duty of care and duty of loyalty.
- A company's board of directors typically has several committees that are responsible for specific functions and report to the board. Although the types of committees may vary across organization, the most common are the audit committee, governance committee, remuneration (compensation) committee, nomination committee, risk committee, and investment committee.
- Stakeholder relationships and corporate governance are continually shaped and influenced by a variety of market and non-market factors.
- Shareholder engagement by a company can provide benefits that include building support against short-term activist investors, countering negative recommendations from proxy advisory firms, and receiving greater support for management's position.
- Shareholder activism encompasses a range of strategies that may be used by shareholders when seeking to compel a company to act in a desired manner.
- From a corporation's perspective, risks of poor governance include weak control systems; ineffective decision making; and legal, regulatory, reputational, and default risk. Benefits include better operational efficiency, control, and operating and financial performance, as well as lower default risk (or cost of debt).
- Key analyst considerations in corporate governance and stakeholder management include economic ownership and voting control, board of directors representation, remuneration and company performance, investor composition, strength of shareholders' rights, and the management of long-term risks.
- ESG integration is the practice of considering environmental, social, and governance factors in the investment process.
- Several terms—sometimes interchangeable—have evolved in relation to ESG integration: sustainable investing, responsible investing, socially responsible investing, and impact investing.
- Negative screening is a type of investment strategy that excludes certain companies or sectors from investment consideration because of their underlying business activities or other environmental or social concerns. Positive screening and best-in-class strategies focus on investments with favorable ESG aspects. Thematic investing focuses on a single factor, such as energy efficiency or climate change.

REFRESHER READING • 2017 • LEVEL II

Financial Statement Analysis

Integration of Financial Statement Analysis Techniques

by Jack T. Ciesielski, Jr., CPA, CFA

Jack T. Ciesielski, Jr., CPA, CFA, is at R.G. Associates, Inc., publisher of The Analyst's Accounting Observer (USA).

LEARNING OUTCOMES

Mastery	*The candidate should be able to:*
☐	**a.** demonstrate the use of a framework for the analysis of financial statements, given a particular problem, question, or purpose (e.g., valuing equity based on comparables, critiquing a credit rating, obtaining a comprehensive picture of financial leverage, evaluating the perspectives given in management's discussion of financial results);
☐	**b.** identify financial reporting choices and biases that affect the quality and comparability of companies' financial statements and explain how such biases may affect financial decisions;
☐	**c.** evaluate the quality of a company's financial data and recommend appropriate adjustments to improve quality and comparability with similar companies, including adjustments for differences in accounting standards, methods, and assumptions;
☐	**d.** evaluate how a given change in accounting standards, methods, or assumptions affects financial statements and ratios;
☐	**e.** analyze and interpret how balance sheet modifications, earnings normalization, and cash flow statement related modifications affect a company's financial statements, financial ratios, and overall financial condition.

INTRODUCTION

It is important to keep in mind that financial analysis is a means to an end and not the end itself. Rather than try to apply every possible technique and tool to every situation, it is essential for the investor to consider and identify the proper type of analysis to apply in a given situation.

The primary reason for performing financial analysis is to help in making an economic decision. Before making such decisions as whether to lend to a particular long-term borrower or to invest a large sum in a common stock, venture capital vehicle, or private equity candidate, an investor or financial decision-maker wants to make sure that the probability of a successful outcome is on his or her side. Rather than leave outcomes to chance, a financial decision-maker should use financial analysis to identify and make more visible potential favorable and unfavorable outcomes.

The purpose of this reading is to provide examples of the effective use of financial analysis in decision making. The framework for the analysis is shown in Exhibit 1. Each case study is set in a different type of company and has a different focus/purpose and context for the analysis. However, each case study follows the basic framework shown in Exhibit 1.

Exhibit 1 A Financial Statement Analysis Framework

Phase	Sources of Information	Examples of Output
Define the purpose and context of the analysis.	■ The nature of the analyst's function, such as evaluating an equity or debt investment or issuing a credit rating ■ Communication with client or supervisor on needs and concerns ■ Institutional guidelines related to developing specific work product	■ Statement of the purpose or objective of the analysis ■ A list (written or unwritten) of specific questions to be answered by the analysis ■ Nature and content of report to be provided ■ Timetable and budgeted resources for completion
Collect input data.	■ Financial statements, other financial data, questionnaires, and industry/economic data ■ Discussions with management, suppliers, customers, and competitors ■ Company site visits (e.g., to production facilities or retail stores)	■ Organized financial statements ■ Financial data tables ■ Completed questionnaires, if applicable
Process input data, as required, into analytically useful data.	■ Data from the previous phase	■ Adjusted financial statements ■ Common-size statements ■ Ratios and graphs ■ Forecasts
Analyze/interpret the data.	■ Input data and processed data	■ Analytical results
Develop and communicate conclusions and recommendations (e.g., with an analysis report).	■ Analytical results and previous reports ■ Institutional guidelines for published reports	■ Analytical report answering questions posed in Phase 1 ■ Recommendation regarding the purpose of the analysis, such as whether to make an investment or grant credit
Follow-up.	■ Information gathered by periodically repeating above steps, as necessary, to determine whether changes to holdings or recommendations are necessary	■ Updated reports and recommendations

SUMMARY

The case studies demonstrate the use of a financial analysis framework in investment decision making. Although the different focus, purpose, and context for each analysis may result in the application of different techniques and tools, each case demonstrates the use of a common financial statement analysis framework. The analysts in the cases start with a global, summarized view of a company and its attributes and dig below the surface of the financial statements to find economic truths that are not apparent from a superficial review. In the case of Nestlé, the analyst applied disaggregation techniques to review the company's performance in terms of ROE and then successively examined the drivers of ROE in increasing detail to evaluate management's skills in capital allocation. In the case of Publicis Groupe, the analyst worked from the opposite direction: The global view presented in the balance sheet lacked information about rights and obligations, and the analyst was able to amplify the balance sheet by estimating a different lease accounting scenario.

In each case, an economic decision is reached, which is consistent with the primary reason for performing financial analysis: to facilitate an economic decision.

Derivatives

Pricing and Valuation of Forward Commitments

by Robert E. Brooks, PhD, CFA, and Barbara Valbuzzi, CFA

Robert E. Brooks, PhD, CFA, is at the University of Alabama (USA). Barbara Valbuzzi, CFA (Italy).

LEARNING OUTCOMES

Mastery	*The candidate should be able to:*
☐	**a.** describe and compare how equity, interest rate, fixed-income, and currency forward and futures contracts are priced and valued;
☐	**b.** calculate and interpret the no-arbitrage value of equity, interest rate, fixed-income, and currency forward and futures contracts;
☐	**c.** describe and compare how interest rate, currency, and equity swaps are priced and valued;
☐	**d.** calculate and interpret the no-arbitrage value of interest rate, currency, and equity swaps.

INTRODUCTION

Forward commitments cover forwards, futures, and swaps. Pricing and valuation of forward commitments will be introduced here. A forward commitment is a derivative instrument in the form of a contract that provides the ability to lock in a price or rate at which one can buy or sell the underlying instrument at some future date or exchange an agreed-upon amount of money at a series of dates. As many investments can be viewed as a portfolio of forward commitments, this material is important to the practice of investment management.

SUMMARY

This reading on forward commitment pricing and valuation provides a foundation for understanding how forwards, futures, and swaps are both priced and valued.

Key points include the following:

- The arbitrageur would rather have more money than less and abides by two fundamental rules: Do not use your own money, and do not take any price risk.
- The no-arbitrage approach is used for the pricing and valuation of forward commitments and is built on the key concept of the law of one price, which states that if two investments have the same future cash flows, regardless of what happens in the future, these two investments should have the same current price.
- Throughout this reading, the following key assumptions are made:
  - Replicating instruments are identifiable and investable.
  - Market frictions are nil.
  - Short selling is allowed with full use of proceeds.
  - Borrowing and lending is available at a known risk-free rate.
- Carry arbitrage models used for forward commitment pricing and valuation are based on the no-arbitrage approach.
- With forward commitments, there is a distinct difference between pricing and valuation; pricing involves the determination of the appropriate fixed price or rate, and valuation involves the determination of the contract's current value expressed in currency units.
- Forward commitment pricing results in determining a price or rate such that the forward contract value is equal to zero.
- The price of a forward commitment is a function of the price of the underlying instrument, financing costs, and other carry costs and benefits.
- With equities, currencies, and fixed-income securities, the forward price is determined such that the initial forward value is zero.
- With forward rate agreements, the fixed interest rate is determined such that the initial value of the FRA is zero.
- Futures contract pricing here can essentially be treated the same as forward contract pricing.
- Because of daily marking to market, futures contract values are zero after each daily settlement.
- The general approach to pricing and valuing swaps as covered here is using a replicating or hedge portfolio of comparable instruments.
- With a basic understanding of pricing and valuing a simple interest rate swap, it is a straightforward extension to pricing and valuing currency swaps and equity swaps.
- With interest rate swaps and some equity swaps, pricing involves solving for the fixed interest rate.
- With currency swaps, pricing involves solving for the two fixed rates as well as the notional amounts in each currency.

Derivatives

Valuation of Contingent Claims

by Robert E. Brooks, PhD, CFA, and David Maurice Gentle, MEc, BSc, CFA

Robert E. Brooks, PhD, CFA, is at the University of Alabama (USA). David Maurice Gentle, MEc, BSc, CFA, is at Omega Risk Consulting (Australia).

LEARNING OUTCOMES

Mastery	*The candidate should be able to*
☐	**a.** describe and interpret the binomial option valuation model and its component terms;
☐	**b.** calculate the no-arbitrage values of European and American options using a two-period binomial model;
☐	**c.** identify an arbitrage opportunity involving options and describe the related arbitrage;
☐	**d.** describe how interest rate options are valued using a two-period binomial model;
☐	**e.** calculate and interpret the value of an interest rate option using a two-period binomial model;
☐	**f.** describe how the value of a European option can be analyzed as the present value of the option's expected payoff at expiration;
☐	**g.** identify assumptions of the Black–Scholes–Merton option valuation model;
☐	**h.** interpret the components of the Black–Scholes–Merton model as applied to call options in terms of a leveraged position in the underlying;
☐	**i.** describe how the Black–Scholes–Merton model is used to value European options on equities and currencies;
☐	**j.** describe how the Black model is used to value European options on futures;
☐	**k.** describe how the Black model is used to value European interest rate options and European swaptions;
☐	**l.** interpret each of the option Greeks;
☐	**m.** describe how a delta hedge is executed;
☐	**n.** describe the role of gamma risk in options trading;
☐	**o.** define implied volatility and explain how it is used in options trading.

INTRODUCTION

A contingent claim is a derivative instrument that provides its owner a right but not an obligation to a payoff determined by an underlying asset, rate, or other derivative. Contingent claims include options, the valuation of which is the objective of this reading. Because many investments contain embedded options, understanding this material is vital for investment management.

Our primary purpose is to understand how the values of options are determined. Option values, as with the values of all financial instruments, are typically obtained using valuation models. Any financial valuation model takes certain inputs and turns them into an output that tells us the fair value or price. Option valuation models, like their counterparts in the forward, futures, and swaps markets, are based on the principle of no arbitrage, meaning that the appropriate price of an option is the one that makes it impossible for any party to earn an arbitrage profit at the expense of any other party. The price that precludes arbitrage profits is the value of the option. Using that concept, we then proceed to introduce option valuation models using two approaches. The first approach is the binomial model, which is based on discrete time, and the second is the Black–Scholes–Merton (BSM) model, which is based on continuous time.

SUMMARY

This reading on the valuation of contingent claims provides a foundation for understanding how a variety of different options are valued. Key points include the following:

- The arbitrageur would rather have more money than less and abides by two fundamental rules: Do not use your own money and do not take any price risk.
- The no-arbitrage approach is used for option valuation and is built on the key concept of the law of one price, which says that if two investments have the same future cash flows regardless of what happens in the future, then these two investments should have the same current price.
- Throughout this reading, the following key assumptions are made:
  - Replicating instruments are identifiable and investable.
  - Market frictions are nil.
  - Short selling is allowed with full use of proceeds.
  - The underlying instrument price follows a known distribution.
  - Borrowing and lending is available at a known risk-free rate.
- The two-period binomial model can be viewed as three one-period binomial models, one positioned at Time 0 and two positioned at Time 1.
- In general, European-style options can be valued based on the expectations approach in which the option value is determined as the present value of the expected future option payouts, where the discount rate is the risk-free rate and the expectation is taken based on the risk-neutral probability measure.
- Both American-style options and European-style options can be valued based on the no-arbitrage approach, which provides clear interpretations of the component terms; the option value is determined by working backward through the binomial tree to arrive at the correct current value.

- For American-style options, early exercise influences the option values and hedge ratios as one works backward through the binomial tree.
- Interest rate option valuation requires the specification of an entire term structure of interest rates, so valuation is often estimated via a binomial tree.
- A key assumption of the Black–Scholes–Merton option valuation model is that the return of the underlying instrument follows geometric Brownian motion, implying a lognormal distribution of the return.
- The BSM model can be interpreted as a dynamically managed portfolio of the underlying instrument and zero-coupon bonds.
- BSM model interpretations related to $N(d_1)$ are that it is the basis for the number of units of underlying instrument to replicate an option, that it is the primary determinant of delta, and that it answers the question of how much the option value will change for a small change in the underlying.
- BSM model interpretations related to $N(d_2)$ are that it is the basis for the number of zero-coupon bonds to acquire to replicate an option and that it is the basis for estimating the risk-neutral probability of an option expiring in the money.
- The Black futures option model assumes the underlying is a futures or a forward contract.
- Interest rate options can be valued based on a modified Black futures option model in which the underlying is a forward rate agreement (FRA), there is an accrual period adjustment as well as an underlying notional amount, and that care must be given to day-count conventions.
- An interest rate cap is a portfolio of interest rate call options termed caplets, each with the same exercise rate and with sequential maturities.
- An interest rate floor is a portfolio of interest rate put options termed floorlets, each with the same exercise rate and with sequential maturities.
- A swaption is an option on a swap.
- A payer swaption is an option on a swap to pay fixed and receive floating.
- A receiver swaption is an option on a swap to receive fixed and pay floating.
- Long a callable fixed-rate bond can be viewed as long a straight fixed-rate bond and short a receiver swaption.
- Delta is a static risk measure defined as the change in a given portfolio for a given small change in the value of the underlying instrument, holding everything else constant.
- Delta hedging refers to managing the portfolio delta by entering additional positions into the portfolio.
- A delta neutral portfolio is one in which the portfolio delta is set and maintained at zero.
- A change in the option price can be estimated with a delta approximation.
- Because delta is used to make a linear approximation of the non-linear relationship that exists between the option price and the underlying price, there is an error that can be estimated by gamma.
- Gamma is a static risk measure defined as the change in a given portfolio delta for a given small change in the value of the underlying instrument, holding everything else constant.
- Gamma captures the non-linearity risk or the risk—via exposure to the underlying—that remains once the portfolio is delta neutral.
- A gamma neutral portfolio is one in which the portfolio gamma is maintained at zero.

- The change in the option price can be better estimated by a delta-plus-gamma approximation compared with just a delta approximation.
- Theta is a static risk measure defined as the change in the value of an option given a small change in calendar time, holding everything else constant.
- Vega is a static risk measure defined as the change in a given portfolio for a given small change in volatility, holding everything else constant.
- Rho is a static risk measure defined as the change in a given portfolio for a given small change in the risk-free interest rate, holding everything else constant.
- Although historical volatility can be estimated, there is no objective measure of future volatility.
- Implied volatility is the BSM model volatility that yields the market option price.
- Implied volatility is a measure of future volatility, whereas historical volatility is a measure of past volatility.
- Option prices reflect the beliefs of option market participant about the future volatility of the underlying.
- The volatility smile is a two dimensional plot of the implied volatility with respect to the exercise price.
- The volatility surface is a three dimensional plot of the implied volatility with respect to both expiration time and exercise prices.
- If the BSM model assumptions were true, then one would expect to find the volatility surface flat, but in practice, the volatility surface is not flat.

REFRESHER READING • 2017 • LEVEL II

Derivatives

Derivatives Strategies

by Robert A. Strong, PhD, CFA, and Russell A. Rhoads, CFA

Robert A. Strong, PhD, CFA, is at the University of Maine (USA). Russell A. Rhoads, CFA, is at The Options Institute at CBOE (USA).

LEARNING OUTCOMES

Mastery	*The candidate should be able to:*
☐	**a.** describe how interest rate, currency, and equity swaps, futures, and forwards can be used to modify risk and return;
☐	**b.** describe how to replicate an asset by using options and by using cash plus forwards or futures;
☐	**c.** describe the investment objectives, structure, payoff, and risk(s) of a covered call position;
☐	**d.** describe the investment objectives, structure, payoff, and risks(s) of a protective put position;
☐	**e.** calculate and interpret the value at expiration, profit, maximum profit, maximum loss, and breakeven underlying price at expiration for covered calls and protective puts;
☐	**f.** contrast protective put and covered call positions to being long an asset and short a forward on the asset;
☐	**g.** describe the investment objective(s), structure, payoffs, and risks of the following option strategies: bull spread, bear spread, collar, and straddle;
☐	**h.** calculate and interpret the value at expiration, profit, maximum profit, maximum loss, and breakeven underlying price at expiration of the following option strategies: bull spread, bear spread, collar, and straddle;
☐	**i.** describe uses of calendar spreads;
☐	**j.** identify and evaluate appropriate derivatives strategies consistent with given investment objectives.

INTRODUCTION

There are many ways in which investors and financial managers routinely use put and call options, futures, forward contracts, and various types of swap contracts to modify their investment positions or to implement market strategies. Some derivative strategies are purely speculative, designed to profit if a particular market change occurs. Other strategies are defensive, providing protection against an adverse event or removing the uncertainty around future events.

The purpose of this reading is to illustrate ways in which derivatives might be used in typical investment situations. Few financial managers or individual investors will ever use all of the strategies described here. That does not mean that some strategies are not important. An informed investment professional should still be aware of them and understand the associated risk–return trade-off. Although part of the medical school curriculum, many physicians will never treat a patient for frostbite or malaria. Regardless, patients have a right to expect that their doctors have an idea about how these conditions might be treated or, better yet, prevented. Someone who is travelling to an area where malaria is prevalent wants to acquire protection before the trip, and we expect doctors to know how to prescribe something for that even if they have never done it before. The doctor may also choose to refer the patient to a specialist, just as an investment manager may need to confer with a derivatives specialist.

An investment manager may not currently use derivatives but should be sufficiently familiar with them that he or she can answer questions about them and explain how they might logically be used to benefit a corporate treasury or protect an investment portfolio. When a financial adviser deals with a client's money, the adviser is dealing with the long-term financial health of the client. Physicians are expected to be current and knowledgeable, and investors have a right to expect the same of their financial advisers.

SUMMARY

This reading on derivatives strategies shows a number of ways in which market participants might use derivatives to enhance returns or to reduce risk to better meet portfolio objectives. The following are the key points.

- Interest rate, currency, and equity futures and swaps can be used to modify risk and return by altering the characteristics of the cash flows of an investment portfolio.
- Buying a call and writing a put with the same exercise price creates a synthetic long position.
- A long position plus a short futures position in the same underlying asset creates a synthetic risk-free asset earning the risk-free rate.
- A covered call, in which the holder of a stock writes a call giving someone the right to buy the shares, is one of the most common uses of options by individual investors.
- Covered calls can be used to generate income, to acquire shares at a lower-than-market price, or to exit a position when the shares hit a target price.
- A covered call position has a limited maximum return because of the transfer of the right tail of the return distribution to the option buyer.

- The maximum loss of a covered call position is less than the maximum loss of the underlying shares alone, but the covered call carries the potential for an opportunity loss if the underlying shares rise sharply.
- A protective put is the simultaneous holding of a long stock position and a long put on the same asset. The put provides protection or insurance against a price decline.
- Although the continuous purchase of protective puts is expensive and probably suboptimal, the occasional purchase of a protective put to deal with a bearish short-term outlook can be a reasonable risk-reducing activity.
- The maximum loss with a protective put is limited because the downside risk is transferred to the option writer in exchange for the payment of the option premium.
- With an option spread, an investor buys one option and writes another of the same type. This reduces the position cost but caps the maximum payoff.
- A bull spread is normally constructed by buying a call option and writing another call option with a higher exercise price.
- A bear spread is normally constructed by buying a put option and writing another put option with a lower exercise price.
- With either a bull spread or a bear spread, both the maximum gain and the maximum loss are known and limited.
- A collar is an option position in which the investor is long shares of stock and simultaneously writes a covered call and buys a protective put.
- A calendar spread involves buying a long-dated option and writing a shorter-dated option of the same type with the same exercise price, or vice versa. The primary motivation for such a spread is to take advantage of the faster time decay with the shorter-term option.
- A straddle is an option combination in which the investor buys puts and calls with the same exercise price. The straddle holder typically needs a substantial price movement in the underlying asset in order to make a profit.
- The risk of a derivative product depends on how it is used. Derivatives should always be used in connection with a well-defined investment objective.

Alternative Investments

Commodities and Commodity Derivatives: An Introduction

by David Burkart, CFA, and James Alan Finnegan, RMA, CFA

David Burkart, CFA, is at Coloma Capital Futures, LLC (USA). James Alan Finnegan, RMA, CFA (USA).

LEARNING OUTCOMES

Mastery	The candidate should be able to
☐	**a.** compare characteristics of commodity sectors;
☐	**b.** compare the life cycle of commodity sectors from production through trading or consumption;
☐	**c.** contrast the valuation of commodities with the valuation of equities and bonds;
☐	**d.** describe types of participants in commodity futures markets;
☐	**e.** analyze the relationship between spot prices and expected future prices in markets in contango and markets in backwardation;
☐	**f.** compare theories of commodity futures returns;
☐	**g.** describe, calculate, and interpret the components of total return for a fully collateralized commodity futures contract;
☐	**h.** contrast roll return in markets in contango and markets in backwardation;
☐	**i.** describe how commodity swaps are used to obtain or modify exposure to commodities;
☐	**j.** describe how the construction of commodity indexes affects index returns.

INTRODUCTION

This reading presents the characteristics and valuation of commodities and commodity derivatives. Given that investment in commodities is conducted primarily through futures markets, the concepts and theories behind commodity futures is a primary focus of the reading. In particular, the relationship between spot and futures prices, as well as the underlying components of futures returns, are key analytical considerations.

What do we mean when we talk about investing in commodities? A basic economic definition is that a commodity is a physical good attributable to a natural resource that is tradable and supplied without substantial differentiation by the general public.

Commodities trade in physical (spot) markets and in futures and forward markets. Spot markets involve the physical transfer of goods between buyers and sellers; prices in these markets reflect current (or very near term) supply and demand conditions. Global commodity futures markets constitute financial exchanges of standardized futures contracts in which a price is established in the market today for the sale of some defined quantity and quality of a commodity at a future date of delivery; execution of the contract may be focused on cash settlement or physical delivery.

Commodity futures exchanges allow for risk transfer and provide a valuable price discovery mechanism that reflects the collective views of all market participants with regard to the future supply and demand prospects of a commodity. Given the financial (versus physical) nature of their contract execution, commodity exchanges allow important parties beyond traditional suppliers and buyers—speculators, arbitrageurs, private equity, endowments, and other institutional investors—to participate in these price discovery and risk transfer processes. Standardized contracts and organized exchanges also offer liquidity (i.e., trading volumes) to facilitate closing, reducing, expanding, or opening new hedges or exposures as circumstances change on a daily basis.

Forward markets exist alongside futures markets in certain commodities for use by entities that require customization in contract terms. Forwards are largely outside the scope of this reading and discussed only briefly. Exposure to commodities is also traded in the swap markets for both speculative and hedging purposes. Investment managers may want to establish swap positions to match certain portfolio needs, whereas producers may want to adjust their commodity risk (e.g., the origin of their cattle or the chemical specifications of their crude oil).

Commodities offer the potential for diversification benefits in a multi-asset class portfolio because of historically low average return correlation with stocks and bonds. In addition, certain academic studies (e.g., Gorton and Rouwenhorst 2006; Erb and Harvey 2006) demonstrate that some commodities have historically had inflation hedging qualities.

SUMMARY

- Commodities are a diverse asset class comprised of various sectors: energy, grains, industrial (base) metals, livestock, precious metals, and softs (cash crops). Each of these sectors has a number of characteristics that are important in determining the supply and demand for each commodity, including ease of storage, geo-politics, and weather.

- The life cycle of commodities varies considerably depending on the economic, technical and structural (i.e., industry, value chain) profile of each commodity as well as the sector. A short life cycle allows for relatively rapid adjustment to outside events, whereas a long life cycle generally limits the ability of the market to react.
- The valuation of commodities relative to that of equities and bonds can be summarized by noting that equities and bonds represent financial assets whereas commodities are physical assets. The valuation of commodities is not based on the estimation of future profitability and cash flows but rather on a discounted forecast of future possible prices based on such factors as the supply and demand of the physical item.
- The commodity trading environment is similar to other asset classes, with three types of trading participants: (1) informed investors/hedgers, (2) speculators, and (3) arbitrageurs.
- Commodities have two general pricing forms: spot prices in the physical markets and futures prices for later delivery. The spot price is the current price to deliver or purchase a physical commodity at a specific location. A futures price is an exchange-based price agreed on to deliver or receive a defined quantity and often quality of a commodity at a future date.
- The difference between spot and futures prices is generally called the basis. When the spot price is higher than the futures price, it is called backwardation, and when it is lower it is called contango. Backwardation and contango are also used to describe the relationship between two futures contracts of the same commodity.
- Commodity contracts can be settled by either cash or physical delivery.
- There are three primary theories of futures returns.
  - In Insurance Theory, commodity producers who are long the physical good are motived to sell the commodity for future delivery to hedge their production price risk exposure.
  - The Hedging Pressure Hypothesis describes when producers along with consumers seek to protect themselves from commodity market price volatility by entering into price hedges to stabilize their projected profits and cash flow.
  - The Theory of Storage focuses on supply and demand dynamics of commodity inventories, including the concept of "convenience yield."
- The total return of a fully collateralized commodity futures contract can be quantified as the spot price return plus the roll return plus the collateral return (risk-free rate return).
- The roll return is effectively the weighted accounting difference (in percentage terms) between the near-term commodity futures contract price and the farther-term commodity futures contract price.
- A commodity swap is a legal contract calling for the exchange of payments over multiple dates as determined by several reference prices or indexes.
- The most relevant commodity swaps include excess return swaps, total return swaps, basis swaps, and variance/volatility swaps.
- The five primary commodity indexes based on assets are (1) the S&P GSCI; (2) the Bloomberg Commodity Index, formerly the Dow Jones–UBS Commodity Index; (3) the Deutsche Bank Liquid Commodity Index; (4) the Thomson Reuters/CoreCommodity CRB Index; and (5) the Rogers International Commodities Index.
- The key differentiating characteristics of commodity indexes are

- the breadth and selection methodology of coverage (number of commodities and sectors) included in each index, noting that some commodities have multiple reference contracts.
- the relative weightings assigned to each component/commodity, and the related methodology for how these weights are determined.
- the methodology and frequency for rolling the individual futures contracts.
- the methodology and frequency for rebalancing the weights of the individual commodities and sectors.
- the governance that determines which commodities are selected.

REFRESHER READING • 2017 • LEVEL II

Risk Management

Measuring and Managing Market Risk

by Don M. Chance, PhD, CFA, and Michelle McCarthy

Don M. Chance, PhD, CFA, is at Louisiana State University (USA). Michelle McCarthy is at Nuveen Investments (USA).

LEARNING OUTCOMES

Mastery	*The candidate should be able to:*
☐	**a.** explain the use of value at risk (VaR) in measuring portfolio risk;
☐	**b.** compare the parametric (variance–covariance), historical simulation, and Monte Carlo simulation methods for estimating VaR;
☐	**c.** estimate and interpret VaR under the parametric, historical simulation, and Monte Carlo simulation methods;
☐	**d.** describe advantages and limitations of VaR;
☐	**e.** describe extensions of VaR;
☐	**f.** describe sensitivity risk measures and scenario risk measures and compare these measures to VaR;
☐	**g.** demonstrate how equity, fixed-income, and options exposure measures may be used in measuring and managing market risk and volatility risk;
☐	**h.** describe the use of sensitivity risk measures and scenario risk measures;
☐	**i.** describe advantages and limitations of sensitivity risk measures and scenario risk measures;
☐	**j.** describe risk measures used by banks, asset managers, pension funds, and insurers;
☐	**k.** explain constraints used in managing market risks, including risk budgeting, position limits, scenario limits, and stop-loss limits;
☐	**l.** explain how risk measures may be used in capital allocation decisions.

INTRODUCTION

This reading is an introduction to the process of measuring and managing market risk. Market risk is the risk that arises from movements in stock prices, interest rates, exchange rates, and commodity prices. Market risk is distinguished from credit risk, which is the risk of loss from the failure of a counterparty to make a promised payment, and also from a number of other risks that organizations face, such as breakdowns in their operational procedures. In essence, market risk is the risk arising from changes in the markets to which an organization has exposure.

Risk management is the process of identifying and measuring risk and ensuring that the risks being taken are consistent with the desired risks. The process of managing market risk relies heavily on the use of models. A model is a simplified representation of a real world phenomenon. Financial models attempt to capture the important elements that determine prices and sensitivities in financial markets. In doing so, they provide critical information necessary to manage investment risk. For example, investment risk models help a portfolio manager understand how much the value of the portfolio is likely to change given a change in a certain risk factor. They also provide insight into the gains and losses the portfolio might reasonably be expected to experience and the frequency with which large losses might occur.

Effective risk management, though, is much more than just applying financial models; it requires the application of judgment and experience not only to know how to use the models appropriately, but also to appreciate the strengths and limitations of the models and to know when to supplement or substitute one model with another model or approach.

Financial markets operate more or less continuously and new prices are constantly being generated. As a result, there is a large amount of data on market risk and a lot of collective experience dealing with this risk, making market risk one of the easier financial risks to analyze. Still, market risk is not an easy risk to capture. Although a portfolio's exposures can be identified with some certainty, the potential losses that could arise from those exposures are unknown. The data used to estimate potential losses are generated from past prices and rates, not the ones to come. Risk management models allow the experienced risk manager to blend that historical data with their own forward-looking judgment and they provide a framework within which to test that judgment.

SUMMARY

This reading on market risk management models covers various techniques used to manage the risk arising from market fluctuations in prices and rates. The key points are summarized as follows.

- Value at risk (VaR) is the minimum loss in either currency units or as a percentage of portfolio value that would be expected to be incurred a certain percentage of the time over a certain period of time given assumed market conditions.
- VaR requires the decomposition of portfolio performance into risk factors.
- The three methods of estimating VaR are the parametric method, the historical simulation method, and the Monte Carlo simulation method.

- The parametric method of VaR estimation typically provides a VaR estimate from the left tail of a normal distribution, incorporating the expected returns, variances, and covariances of the components of the portfolio.
- The parametric method exploits the simplicity of the normal distribution but provides a poor estimate of VaR when returns are not normally distributed, as might occur when a portfolio contains options.
- The historical simulation method of VaR estimation uses historical return data on the portfolio's current holdings and allocation.
- The historical simulation method has the advantage of incorporating events that actually occurred and does not require the specification of a distribution or the estimation of parameters, but it is only useful to the extent that the future resembles the past.
- The Monte Carlo simulation method of VaR estimation requires the specification of a statistical distribution of returns and the generation of random outcomes from that distribution.
- The Monte Carlo simulation method is extremely flexible but can be complex and time consuming to use.
- There is no single right way of estimating VaR.
- The advantages of VaR include the following: It is a simple concept; it is relatively easy to understand; it is easily communicated, capturing much information in a single number; it can be useful in comparing risks across asset classes, portfolios, and trading units and, as such, it facilitates capital allocation decisions; it can be used for performance evaluation; it can be verified by using backtesting; it is widely accepted by regulators.
- The primary limitations of VaR are that it is a subjective measure and highly sensitive to numerous discretionary choices made in the course of computation; it can underestimate the frequency of extreme events; it fails to account for the lack of liquidity; it is sensitive to correlation risk; it is vulnerable to trending or volatility regimes; it is often misunderstood as a worst-case scenario; it can oversimplify the picture of risk; it focuses heavily on the left tail.
- There are numerous variations and extensions of VaR, including conditional VaR (CVaR), incremental VaR (IVaR), and marginal VaR (MVaR) that can provide additional useful information.
- Conditional VaR is the average loss conditional on exceeding the VaR cutoff.
- Incremental VaR measures the change in portfolio VaR as a result of adding or deleting a position from the portfolio or if a position size is changed relative to the remaining positions.
- MVaR measures the change in portfolio VaR given a small change in the portfolio position. In a diversified portfolio, MVaRs can be summed to determine the contribution of each asset to the overall VaR.
- *Ex ante* tracking error measures the degree to which the performance of a given investment portfolio might deviate from its benchmark.
- Sensitivity measures quantify how a security or portfolio will react if a single risk factor changes. Common sensitivity measures are beta for equities; duration and convexity for bonds; and delta, gamma, and vega for options. Sensitivity measures do not indicate which portfolio has greater loss potential.
- Risk managers can use deltas, gammas, vegas, durations, convexities, and betas to get a comprehensive picture of the sensitivity of the entire portfolio.
- Stress tests apply extreme negative stress to a particular portfolio exposure.

- Scenario measures, including stress tests, are risk models that evaluate how a portfolio will perform under certain high-stress market conditions.
- Scenario measures can be based on actual historical scenarios or on hypothetical scenarios.
- Historical scenarios are scenarios that measure the portfolio return that would result from a repeat of a particular period of financial market history.
- Hypothetical scenarios model the impact of extreme movements and co-movements in different markets that have not previously occurred.
- Reverse stress testing is the process of stressing the portfolio's most significant exposures.
- Sensitivity and scenario risk measures can complement VaR; they do not need to rely on history, and scenarios can be designed to overcome an assumption of normal distributions.
- Limitations of scenario measures include the following: Historical scenarios are unlikely to re-occur in exactly the same way; hypothetical scenarios may incorrectly specify how assets will co-move and may get the magnitude of movements wrong; and it is difficult to establish appropriate limits on a scenario analysis or stress test.
- The degree of leverage, the mix of risk factors to which the business is exposed, and accounting or regulatory requirements influence the types of risk measures used by different market participants.
- Banks use risk tools to assess the extent of any liquidity and asset/liability mis-match, the probability of losses in their investment portfolios, their overall leverage ratio, interest rate sensitivities, and the risk to economic capital.
- Asset managers' use of risk tools focus primarily on volatility, probability of loss, or the probability of underperforming a benchmark.
- Pension funds use risk measures to evaluate asset/liability mis-match and surplus at risk.
- Property and casualty insurers use sensitivity and exposure measures to ensure exposures remain within defined asset allocation ranges, economic capital and VaR measures to estimate the impairment in the event of a catastrophic loss, and scenario analysis to stress the market risks and insurance risks simultaneously.
- Life insurers use risk measures to assess the exposures of the investment portfolio and the annuity liability, the extent of any asset/liability mis-match, and the potential stress losses based on the differences between the assets in which they have invested and the liabilities resulting from the insurance contracts they have written.
- Constraints are widely used in risk management in the form of risk budgets, position limits, scenario limits, stop-loss limits, and capital allocation.
- Risk budgeting is the allocation of the total risk appetite across sub-portfolios.
- A scenario limit is a limit on the estimated loss for a given scenario, which, if exceeded, would require corrective action in the portfolio.
- A stop-loss limit requires a reduction in the size of a portfolio, or its complete liquidation, when a loss of a particular size occurs in a specified period.
- Position limits are limits on the market value of any given investment.
- Risk measurements and constraints in and of themselves are not restrictive or unrestrictive; it is the limits placed on the measures that drive action.

Portfolio Management

Algorithmic Trading and High-Frequency Trading

by John Bates, PhD

John Bates, PhD, is at Judge Business School, University of Cambridge (United Kingdom).

LEARNING OUTCOMES

Mastery	The candidate should be able to:
☐	a. define algorithmic trading;
☐	b. distinguish between execution algorithms and high-frequency trading algorithms;
☐	c. describe types of execution algorithms and high-frequency trading algorithms;
☐	d. describe market fragmentation and its effects on how trades are placed;
☐	e. describe the use of technology in risk management and regulatory oversight;
☐	f. describe issues and concerns related to the impact of algorithmic and high-frequency trading on securities markets.

INTRODUCTION

It is estimated that 75% of US stock trades are not placed by humans but by computer algorithms. This figure has been expanding over time and is expected to continue to do so. More trading is done by machines than humans because the human brain cannot process the volumes of information needed to make trading decisions and place trades before a competitor does. Algorithms can process millions of pieces of data per second, make sub-millisecond decisions, and take autonomous actions.

Adapted from a 2010 submission to the CFTC Technology Advisory Committee on Algorithmic and High-Frequency Trading. Dr. Bates is a member of the CFTC Technology Advisory Committee.

A trading algorithm may be as straightforward as an *execution algorithm* that is programmed to intelligently slice up large trades on behalf of a buy-side firm (such as a pension fund or mutual fund) to minimize market impact. But an algorithm can get as complex as a self-learning, *high-frequency algorithm* that makes decisions on what, when, and how to trade and executes these trades itself, without any human input.

It is not just equities that are traded by algorithms; the same algorithmic trading trend is evident in other electronically traded asset classes: futures, foreign exchange (FX), bonds, energy, and so on. In all of these asset classes, algorithms are autonomously managing more and more of the trading decisions. And this trend is occurring in all trading markets around the world. There is, in fact, a high-frequency algorithmic war raging: Algorithms compete to find the best opportunities and execute on them first. This has been a concern to some parties who are worried that certain market participants have an "unfair advantage." But humans are still needed as the creators of algorithms and arbiters of good sense. It has not yet become possible to digitize the instincts of a really good trader!

Algorithms have a life cycle: from research to implementation to testing to tuning. Sometimes algorithms go wrong, which can be extremely costly. There is, therefore, increased interest in using compliance algorithms to monitor trading algorithms, with a view to detecting aberrant behavior.

SUMMARY

Algorithmic and high-frequency trading are important factors in today's markets. Just like electronic terminals replaced open outcry (trading by shouting and waving bits of paper in the trading pits of stock exchanges), so algorithms are replacing the humans that operated the electronic trading terminals in various forms of trade execution. Key points to remember regarding algorithmic trading include the following:

- There are two main types of algorithms: execution algorithms, which minimize the market impact of large orders, and high-frequency algorithms, which constantly monitor real-time market data and look for patterns to trade on.
- Algorithms can adapt to market fragmentation by incorporating liquidity aggregation and intelligent smart order routing capabilities.
- Algorithms can be used for real-time pricing of instruments.
- Low latency is important and latency at each layer of the end-to-end latency equation must be considered: the physical connections to the market, the market data feeds, the algorithmic engine, and the order execution feed to a trading venue.
- The life cycle of an algorithm includes alpha discovery to find new patterns, algorithm implementation, back testing, production, and tuning.
- Algorithms are used in many asset classes, including equities, futures, foreign exchange, bonds, and energy. Algorithms will likely be developed to exploit additional areas as new types of assets migrate to electronic trading.
- Surveillance algorithms can be used to spot potential market abuse and compliance breaches.

- The broad market impact of algorithmic trading is largely positive. Research shows that HFT has led to tighter bid–ask spreads, lower transaction costs, increases in liquidity, and improved pricing efficiency.
- The primary concerns regarding HFT are the potential for HFT to accentuate and accelerate market movements: the risk posed by an out-of-control algorithm, the ability of a trader to manipulate the market through spoofing or quote stuffing, the increased complexity of regulatory oversight, and the impact of unequal access to information.

Private Wealth Management

Risk Management for Individuals

by David M. Blanchett, CFP, CFA, David M. Cordell, PhD, CFP, CFA, Michael S. Finke, PhD, and Thomas Idzorek, CFA

David M. Blanchett, CFP, CFA, is at Morningstar Investment Management (USA). David M. Cordell, PhD, CFP, CFA, is at the University of Texas at Dallas (USA). Michael S. Finke, PhD, is at Texas Tech University (USA). Thomas M. Idzorek, CFA, is at Morningstar (USA).

LEARNING OUTCOMES

Mastery	*The candidate should be able to:*
☐	**a.** compare the characteristics of human capital and financial capital as components of an individual's total wealth;
☐	**b.** discuss the relationships among human capital, financial capital, and net wealth;
☐	**c.** discuss the financial stages of life for an individual;
☐	**d.** describe an economic (holistic) balance sheet;
☐	**e.** discuss risks (earnings, premature death, longevity, property, liability, and health risks) in relation to human and financial capital;
☐	**f.** describe types of insurance relevant to personal financial planning;
☐	**g.** describe the basic elements of a life insurance policy and how insurers price a life insurance policy;
☐	**h.** discuss the use of annuities in personal financial planning;
☐	**i.** discuss the relative advantages and disadvantages of fixed and variable annuities;
☐	**j.** analyze and critique an insurance program;
☐	**k.** discuss how asset allocation policy may be influenced by the risk characteristics of human capital;
☐	**l.** recommend and justify appropriate strategies for asset allocation and risk reduction when given an investor profile of key inputs.

INTRODUCTION

Risk management for individuals is a key element of life-cycle finance, which recognizes that as investors age, the fundamental nature of their total wealth evolves, as do the risks that they face. **Life-cycle finance** is concerned with helping investors achieve their goals, including an adequate retirement income, by taking a holistic view of the individual's financial situation as he or she moves through life. Individuals are exposed to a range of risks over their lives: They may become disabled, suffer a prolonged illness, die prematurely, or outlive their resources. In addition, from an investment perspective, the assets of individuals could decline in value or provide an inadequate return in relation to financial needs and aspirations. All of these risks have two things in common: They are typically random, and they can result in financial hardship without an appropriate risk management strategy. Risk management for individuals is distinct from risk management for corporations given the distinctive characteristics of households, which include the finite and unknown lifespan of individuals, the frequent preference for stable spending among individuals, and the desire to pass on wealth to heirs (i.e., through bequests). To protect against unexpected financial hardships, risks must be identified, market and non-market solutions considered, and a plan developed and implemented. A well-constructed plan for risk management will involve the selection of financial products and investment strategies that fit an individual's financial goals and mitigate the risk of shortfalls.

SUMMARY

The risk management process for individuals is complex given the variety of potential risks that may be experienced over the life cycle and the differences that exist across households. In this reading, key concepts related to risk management and individuals include the following:

- The two primary asset types for most individuals can be described broadly as human capital and financial capital. Human capital is the net present value of the individual's future expected labor income, whereas financial capital consists of assets currently owned by the individual and can include such items as a bank account, individual securities, pooled funds, a retirement account, and a home.
- Net wealth is an extension of net worth that includes claims to future assets that can be used for consumption, such as human capital, as well as the present value of pension benefits.
- There are typically four key steps in the risk management process for individuals: Specify the objective, identify risks, evaluate risks and select appropriate methods to manage the risks, and monitor outcomes and risk exposures and make appropriate adjustments in methods.
- The financial stages of life for adults can be categorized in the following seven periods: education phase, early career, career development, peak accumulation, pre-retirement, early retirement, and late retirement.
- The primary goal of an economic (holistic) balance sheet is to arrive at an accurate depiction of an individual's overall financial health by accounting for the present value of all available marketable and non-marketable assets, as well as all liabilities. An economic (holistic) balance sheet includes traditional assets and liabilities, as well as human capital and pension value, as assets and includes consumption and bequests as liabilities.

- The total economic wealth of an individual changes throughout his or her lifetime, as do the underlying assets that make up that wealth. The total economic wealth of younger individuals is typically dominated by the value of their human capital. As individuals age, earnings will accumulate, increasing financial capital.
- Earnings risk refers to the risks associated with the earnings potential of an individual—that is, events that could negatively affect someone's human and financial capital.
- Premature death risk relates to the death of an individual, such as a family member, whose future earnings (human capital) were expected to help pay for the financial needs and aspirations of the family.
- Longevity risk is the risk of reaching an age at which one's income and financial assets are insufficient to provide adequate support.
- Property risk relates to the possibility that one's property may be damaged, destroyed, stolen, or lost. There are different types of property insurance, depending on the asset, such as automobile insurance and homeowner's insurance.
- Liability risk refers to the possibility that an individual or other entity may be held legally liable for the financial costs of property damage or physical injury.
- Health risk refers to the risks and implications associated with illness or injury. Health risks manifest themselves in different ways over the life cycle and can have significant implications for human capital.
- The primary purpose of life insurance is to help replace the economic value of an individual to a family or a business in the event of that individual's death. The family's need for life insurance is related to the potential loss associated with the future earnings power of that individual.
- The two main types of life insurance are temporary and permanent. Temporary life insurance, or term life insurance, provides insurance for a certain period of time specified at purchase, whereas permanent insurance, or whole life insurance, is used to provide lifetime coverage, assuming the premiums are paid over the entire period.
- Fixed annuities provide a benefit that is fixed (or known) for life, whereas variable annuities have a benefit that can change over time and that is generally based on the performance of some underlying portfolio or investment. When selecting between fixed and variable annuities, there are a number of important considerations, such as the volatility of the benefit, flexibility, future market expectations, fees, and inflation concerns.
- Among the factors that would likely increase demand for an annuity are the following: longer-than-average life expectancy, greater preference for lifetime income, less concern for leaving money to heirs, more conservative investing preferences, and lower guaranteed income from other sources (such as pensions).
- Techniques for managing a risk include risk avoidance, risk reduction, risk transfer, and risk retention. The most appropriate choice among these techniques often is related to consideration of the frequency and severity of losses associated with the risk.
- The decision to retain risk or buy insurance is determined by a household's risk tolerance. At the same level of wealth, a more risk-tolerant household will prefer to retain more risk, either through higher insurance deductibles or by simply not buying insurance, than will a less risk-tolerant household. Insurance products that have a higher load will encourage a household to retain more risk.

- An individual's total economic wealth affects portfolio construction through asset allocation, which includes the overall allocation to risky assets, as well as the underlying asset classes, such as stocks and bonds, selected by the individual.
- Investment risk, property risk, and human capital risk can be either idiosyncratic or systematic. Examples of idiosyncratic risks include the risks of a specific occupation, the risk of living a very long life or experiencing a long-term illness, and the risk of premature death or loss of property. Systematic risks affect all households.

Made in the USA
Monee, IL
05 November 2026

67375664R00036